Facts About the Bison

By Lisa Strattin

© 2019 Lisa Strattin

FREE BOOK

FREE FOR ALL SUBSCRIBERS

LisaStrattin.com/Subscribe-Here

BOX SET

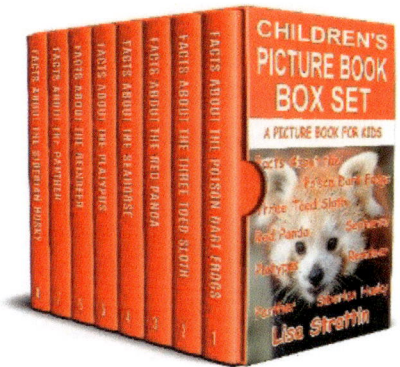

- **FACTS ABOUT THE POISON DART FROGS**
- **FACTS ABOUT THE THREE TOED SLOTH**
  - **FACTS ABOUT THE RED PANDA**
  - **FACTS ABOUT THE SEAHORSE**
  - **FACTS ABOUT THE PLATYPUS**
  - **FACTS ABOUT THE REINDEER**
  - **FACTS ABOUT THE PANTHER**
- **FACTS ABOUT THE SIBERIAN HUSKY**

LisaStrattin.com/BookBundle

Facts for Kids Picture Books by Lisa Strattin

Little Blue Penguin, Vol 92

Chipmunk, Vol 5

Frilled Lizard, Vol 39

Blue and Gold Macaw, Vol 13

Poison Dart Frogs, Vol 50

Blue Tarantula, Vol 115

African Elephants, Vol 8

Amur Leopard, Vol 89

Sabre Tooth Tiger, Vol 167

Baboon, Vol 174

Sign Up for New Release Emails Here

LisaStrattin.com/subscribe-here

All rights reserved. No part of this book may be reproduced by any means whatsoever without the written permission from the author, except brief portions quoted for purpose of review.

All information in this book has been carefully researched and checked for factual accuracy. However, the author and publisher makes no warranty, express or implied, that the information contained herein is appropriate for every individual, situation or purpose and assume no responsibility for errors or omissions. The reader assumes the risk and full responsibility for all actions, and the author will not be held responsible for any loss or damage, whether consequential, incidental, special or otherwise, that may result from the information presented in this book.

All images are free for use or purchased from stock photo sites or royalty free for commercial use.

Some coloring pages might be of the general species due to lack of available images.

I have relied on my own observations as well as many different sources for this book and I have done my best to check facts and give credit where it is due. In the event that any material is used without proper permission, please contact me so that the oversight can be corrected.

COVER IMAGE

https://flickr.com/photos/naturenps/33233259955/

ADDITIONAL IMAGES

https://flickr.com/photos/adombrowski/5908260071/

https://flickr.com/photos/cobaltfish/13564837613/

https://flickr.com/photos/mrfraley/6979075740/

https://flickr.com/photos/schizoform/7699211780/

https://flickr.com/photos/usfwsmtnprairie/5355367784/

https://flickr.com/photos/dougfrancis/7577804714/

https://flickr.com/photos/thimindu/5056190510/

https://flickr.com/photos/yellowstonenps/32523449400/

https://flickr.com/photos/jniola/36680859432/

https://flickr.com/photos/usfwsmidwest/33154296702/

Contents

INTRODUCTION 9

CHARACTERISTICS 11

APPEARANCE 13

LIFE STAGES 15

LIFE SPAN 17

SIZE 19

HABITAT 21

DIET 23

ENEMIES 25

SUITABILITY AS PETS 27

INTRODUCTION

The bison is also known as the American Bison and the American Buffalo, although they are only thought to be very distantly related to the buffalo and the water buffalo which are found in Africa and Asia respectively.

CHARACTERISTICS

The bison is considered to be the largest land mammal in existence in North America, where the natural habitat of the bison ranged from Canada to Mexico. Due to habitat loss and hunting of the bison, they are now only found in large herds in few areas and farmland.

Before the settlers arrived in North America in the 1800s, it is estimated that there were 60 to 100 million bison living in the area, but the settlers hunted the bison population down to just more than 1,000 animals, from which the species has still not fully recovered.

APPEARANCE

The bison is one of the largest types of cow in the world, with adult bison commonly growing to 6.5 feet tall or more. They typically have long shaggy brown hair if they live in colder regions and those in the warmer climates have shorter hair. They have a mane as well as a beard under their chin and a short tail with a tuft of hair at the end of it. They have a large head, short black horns and a hump on their shoulders.

LIFE STAGES

The mother and her calf stay away from the herd for a couple of days. At about two months, the calf begins to develop the shoulder humps and horns. The calf is usually weaned by the time it is seven months old, but it stays with its mother until it is a year old.

LIFE SPAN

Bison generally live for 15-20 years in the wild.

SIZE

Adult bison are 6.5 to 9 feet long and weigh over 2,000 pounds. They are very big!

HABITAT

American bison live in river valleys, and on prairies and plains. Typical habitat is open or semi-open grasslands, as well as sagebrush, semiarid lands, and scrublands.

Large herds of bison once dominated the North American landscape from the Appalachians to the Rockies, from the Gulf Coast to Alaska. Habitat loss and unregulated hunting reduced the population to just over 1,000 animals by 1889. In 2019, approximately 500,000 bison live across North America.

DIET

The American bison is a grazer. Their diet is made up of mostly grasses and sedges, although they will occasionally eat berries and lichen. In the winter months, the bison uses its head and hooves to move snow so they can get to the vegetation beneath.

ENEMIES

The wild bison has been hunted by humans for meat, skins and trophy hunting. They have only a handful of predators in the wild, mainly due to their sheer size. Wolves, bears and cougars are among the animals that will hunt the bison in their natural habitat.

SUITABILITY AS PETS

Although ranchers raise bison, they are not considered pets. They are huge wild animals and not likely to be domesticated. They might be safe enough around people who raise them and know how to treat them, but not for most people.

COLOR ME

COLOR ME

COLOR ME

COLOR ME

COLOR ME

COLOR ME

COLOR ME

COLOR ME

COLOR ME

COLOR ME

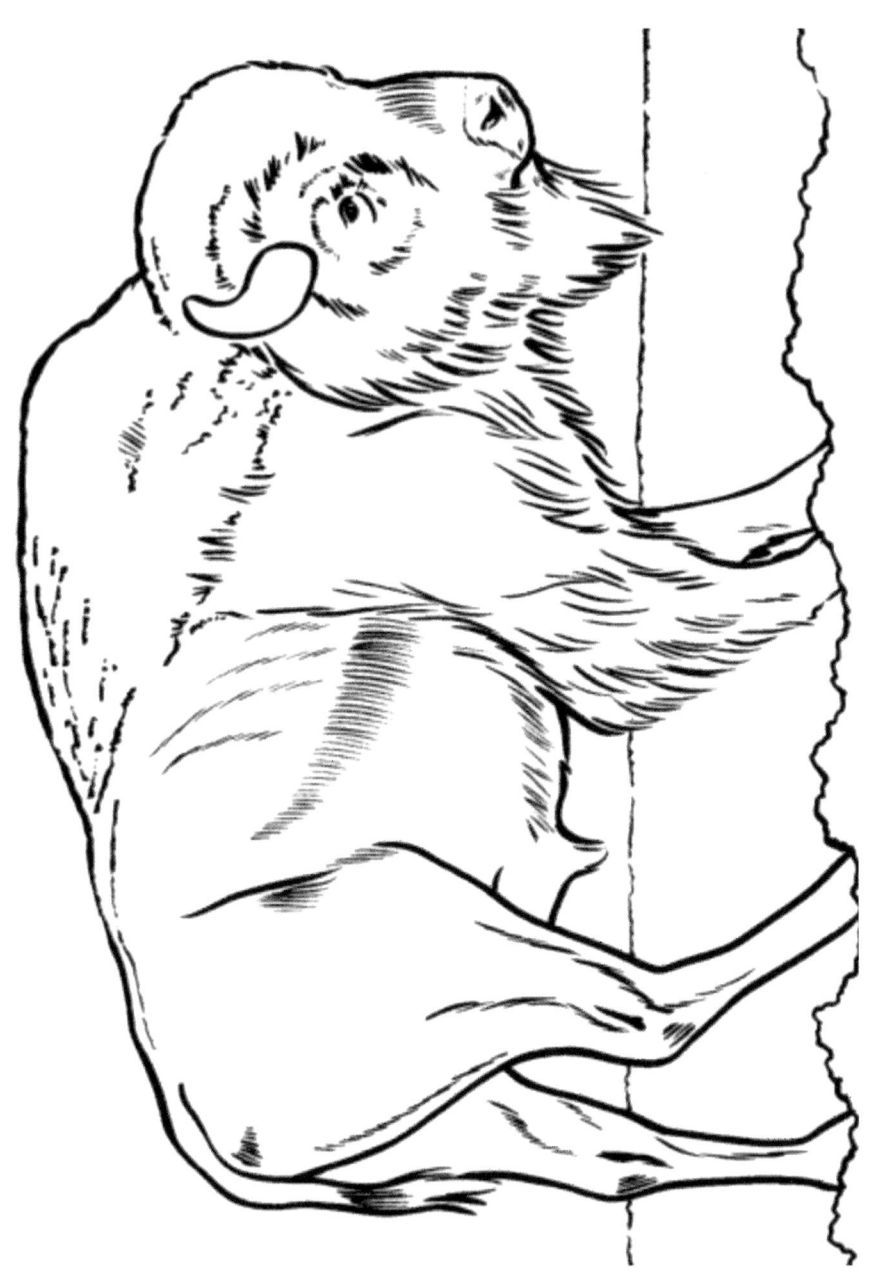

Please leave me a review here:

LisaStrattin.com/Review-Vol-220

For more Kindle Downloads Visit Lisa Strattin Author Page on Amazon Author Central

amazon.com/author/lisastrattin

To see upcoming titles, visit my website at LisaStrattin.com– most books available on Kindle!

LisaStrattin.com

FREE BOOK

FOR ALL SUBSCRIBERS – SIGN UP NOW

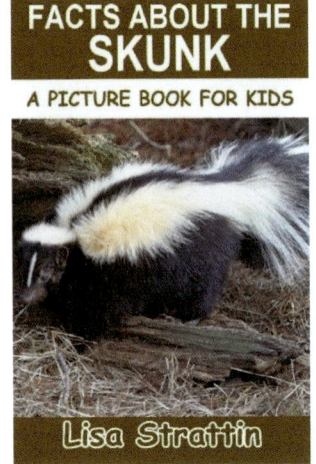

LisaStrattin.com/Subscribe-Here

LisaStrattin.com/Facebook

LisaStrattin.com/Youtube

Printed in Great Britain
by Amazon